MW01356607

This Journal Belongs To:

____

Made in United States
North Haven, CT
30 May 2025

69332156R00067